GOD's PLAN
Rosemarie Metoyer

When the motive of the heart is true love
it changes the outcome.

Edited by Phillip Franklin

Acknowledgement

I would like to acknowledge my good friend Jamie Karis for his undying passion to guide people to the truth through God's word and commitment to Discipleship. I want to thank Phillip Franklin who was gracious enough to help me with editing without changing the message. Their dedication for the truth and love for God has been a great influence in my life. I thank the ladies in my bible study group who have been great women that have supported me and are always looking out for me Tasha, Felisha, Jazmon, Antrica, and Donnisha. I owe gratitude to my good friend Evie Selman who is always praying for me and has walked my journey with me personally and spiritually. To my friends I go to when I need to vent and whose opinions I value, Yolanda Pickett, Curtis Jones and Lori Robinson, I owe much thanks and gratitude.

Finally to my Children Leha, Lathette and Amber who are always looking out for their mom and are my inspiration and loves of my life.

This book is not written to pass judgment or to make anyone feel short of the Glory of our God. It is written with one thing in mind and that is to bring a conscious, intentional, thought-provoking message to check our hearts.

Every now and then we, as believers, need to pause and examine our own hearts to make sure we are aligning our thoughts and actions with the same intentions that Jesus did, which was to fulfill the Plan of God.

I truly hope that we all can "stop, drop, and roll" since we are all so preoccupied with personal goals for our lives, work, family, society, and church. Sometimes these things can be distractions and can cause us to move away from what is most important. For me, what is most important, is that I fulfill the Plan of God through the purpose I was put on this earth for– which is to become a true Disciple of the Most High God and that His will be done on earth as it is in Heaven.

CONTENTS

My Story 1

My Search 4

My Purpose 9

Motive of the Heart 12

Love is the Greatest 14

A Few Testimonies 25

Message to Leaders 38

Freedom from Fear 43

Demonstration as a Tool 45

Loveless Church 47

My Prayer 48

Prayer of Repentance 49

My Story

I want to start off by telling you a little about myself. I have learned how to love the Lord our God with all my heart, mind and soul and I have also learned how to love myself and others (as it states in Mark 12:30-31 NLT). Although I grew up in church most of my life it was not until I started spending time searching for God on my own that I found Him. I remember the day I decided to focus on Him. This was my prayer on that day.

> "God, I want to know you for myself–not through any ministry or through my mother, or father, or sister or brother but for myself–just me and you. I am going to start searching for you no matter what. Whether I am doing the right thing or not, nothing is going to stop me. I am not

God's Plan

> going to allow my life decisions, either bad or good, to stop me from finding out who you are. No more guilt! I am going to simply pursue you because I want to know you."

Well, He heard me and proved that he definitely is a rewarder of those who diligently seek Him (Hebrews 11:6 NLT).

I was born in San Bernardino CA. As a newborn I was adopted but I did not find this out until later in life. In Fact I was told this when I was about 11. My children wanted me to know my bloodline so they purchased Ancestry.com as a gift and there I found who my mother and father are along with many siblings that I have had the pleasure of meeting. I am so grateful because even though I tried not to let it bother me there was an emptiness inside of me. I definitely feel more whole and complete knowing who I am. It also feels good to see people who look like me and to understand why I act like I do. DNA is strong and not only carries physical resemblances but also personality traits.

My Search

One day I called my friend Jamie and told him about my new quest for knowing God. I told him I am not an avid reader but send me some books to help me navigate through the Bible. I told God I wanted to have a "burning bush" experience with him (like Moses did in Exodus 3:1-3 NLT). So I started fasting, praying and reading. I used to walk up to the top of Stone Mountain (near Atlanta GA) every day with my backpack which had my Bible in it, along with headphones for listening to my gospel music. I would sit there and say "God here I am, show me who you are and give me that "burning bush" experience I so desire.

One night I woke up and I looked at my bedroom window and I saw a blue fluorescent thin cross. At first I was scared so I closed my eyes. When I opened them, the cross was still there. I buried my head into my pillow and I said "This cannot be! This cannot be!" and made myself go to sleep. The next morning when I woke up I jumped out of bed and said "this really did happen–I cannot deny it". I called my friend Jamie and I started telling him what happened. Before I could tell him what the cross looked like he said "Was it a blue fluorescent, thin cross?" I said "YES!". He said he saw it last night when he was leaving his girlfriend's apartment. It was on the elevator door and I thought it was a sign from God warning me not to get on the elevators. This was my confirmation that I really saw what I saw. "WOW!". God knew I trusted Jamie and that Jamie was helping me grow into the knowledge. God is so very clever!

From that point on I have been studying the Bible and reading books that help me

God's Plan

understand who God is. I have really and truly fallen in love with Him. I am stronger, wiser and more equipped to share and live this life of kingdom living. I am not perfect but my heart is pure. I try to make every day count. My effort is not because of some pressure but I delight in Him–knowing that He loves me more. As my journey continued, it was not all joy but the hard times paid off and the molding was worth it. I am so glad God will never leave us nor forsake us or condemn us (Deuteronomy 31:8 NLT). He already knew about my behavior and mistakes (Romans 8:1 NLT). He knew I would fall short and He still loved me and made a way for me. His plan for me never stopped, if I could only get you as a reader to understand you are wonderfully and beautifully made with a real plan for your life– a purpose He has put in you while you were in the womb of your mother (Jeremiah 1:5 NLT). His thoughts and plans never changed and this is not because you did or did not deserve it but because he loves you and you have the gift of salvation because you are His.

My adopted mother was a pastor and had a gift to preach, sing, and play the piano and organ. She also had a gift for prayer and I remember hearing her several nights crying out to God in English and in a heavenly tongue. I did not understand then like I do now what she was doing. After my adopted father and mother divorced, my mother moved us to New Jersey where we attended all of the big Pentecostal churches you could think of. I remember being in church and hearing that almost everything you could think of was a sin–pants, makeup, going to parades, movies and the list went on. We traveled to tent revivals and stayed in actual tents with all of the other saints. We were in church all day and all night shouting, singing, and praying with lots of preaching!

God's Plan

My mother worked as a house cleaner. She was an immaculate cleaner of her own home and had the same magic for other homes as well. I used to go with her when I did not go to school and she cleaned the homes of some very rich people. I was amazed at how they lived and it seemed that they had everything. I enjoyed going because I could play with their kids and they were very nice to me. They had toys, games, dolls, and a backyard.

God's Plan

My Purpose

Here is where my story really began, a story of purpose and carrying the torch for righteousness so God may be glorified and His mysterious plans revealed for this season. We often think the only mystery was what Paul spoke about regarding God's plan for salvation for the Jews and the Gentiles but that was just part of the mystery (Ephesians 3:8-9 NLT). The mystery for this season is a continuation of God's plan to bring everything together under the authority of God–everything in heaven and everything on earth. Even all creation waits for this revelation (Romans 8:19-21 NLT).

God speaks to us through signs and wonders and even through our own life experiences but please do not think this is the only way He speaks. He does speak to us in many ways, sometimes it could be in a small voice, or visions, dreams, nature, other people and the list goes on. You see we cannot put God in a box, He is all-knowing and omnipotent with no beginning and no end. He is the Creator and there is no God besides Him. All the power and glory is His forever and ever (Isaiah 45:6 NLT). He made us in His image and there is no end for us. Not even death is an end for us so what do we do in the meantime?

Well, we wait on Him, trust Him and seek Him. He said "seek and you shall find" and that "He is a rewarder of those who diligently seek Him". He wants only the best for His creation and we will experience His power and glory forever and ever (now and for eternity) because this is His plan.

God's Plan

What we must do is become doers of His word and obey Him when He speaks. You see, obedience is better than sacrifice (James 1: 22-25) and we must become doers of His word. Oh how we get this so wrong, we think sacrifice is better and will give us the keys to heaven. We think if we sacrifice enough we will find favor and receive the keys to life with Him and live in his promises. But this is not His way or His plan, He already made the sacrifice through His only begotten son (Galatians 6, read the entire chapter). So now we live with Him, reconciled back to His original plan, to live with Him and in Him and experience His promises. The work has been finished and we have been liberated.

So why do we keep making up stuff like titles, rituals and guidelines???? WHY????????

God's Plan

Motive of the Heart

We keep making people jump through hoops and doctrines and service as if these things are the keys. NO, let's stop showing the world this is the way when it is not. These things are not the way to follow God's already established plan. He is the Alpha and the Omega (the beginning and the end). We need to seek Him and obey Him.

Matters of the heart is what is important now. What is the motive of our heart? Is it to serve God and each other with love? Christ the Messiah taught that the most important commandment is to love God, ourselves and everyone else (Matthew 22:37-40). This love should always be the motive of our hearts. It starts with acknowledging and believing in our hearts and confessing with our mouths because

God's Plan

when you believe something you verbally acknowledge it and you truly believe it with all your heart. Now the journey begins, the walk with God and our purpose unfolds. I used to think, ok, I can love God but how do I love myself? I have done so much wrong. Please stop this thinking it comes from the accuser who comes to kill, steal and destroy God's plan (unsuccessfully I might add). We are to love ourselves because we are made in His image and a special priesthood. Even the angels ask who we are and why He shows so much favor. This is what we can love about ourselves (Psalm 139:13-14). Anything outside of this reality is a lie and we should stop believing it. Yes, God looks at our hearts. He sees all and has made provision for it all.

God's Plan

Love is the Greatest

Love is the greatest gift of all, when all else is gone love still stands forever because it comes from God who is love eternal. I love the way Paul describes and prays for us in Ephesians 3:18 when he states that we may be able to comprehend with all the saints what is the width and length and depth and height, to know the love of Christ which passes knowledge that we may be filled with all the fullness of God. This should always be at the forefront of our motives and actions. To live in this love God has for us and be ambassadors of this love.

We have distorted our thinking about love that it has to be earned, worked for or comes with conditions. It has been perverted by the enemy because he knows if he can get us to think of love outside of the pure, unconditional and

God's Plan

with no condemnation from God, we would live in utter chaos and confusion and be powerless–in fact we would become destructive. Love is not being controlled at any level but freely given with no conditions. You might think "Wow this makes me vulnerable!" but it is quite the opposite. He has made us kings and queens of His Kingdom. He wants us to operate in wisdom and knowledge. God does not want us to be in the dark but in His light. He does not want us to be defeated but more than conquerors. He does not want us to lose in this journey. God's word states that no weapon formed against us shall prosper.

The only way we can know this true love is to seek Him with all of our heart. How do you do this? You do this like you would do anything else humanly possible when you want to know something. Search for Him, spend time with Him and quietly meditate on the messages He has left for us to study. Seek Him and you will find him, knock and the door shall be opened. It is now between you and Him, not church doors, not service in an organization, not through a pastor or anything else but between you and God.

Not to say these things are not helpful but they can be misguided. Did not God shut the doors of the church recently with covid? Did we not just have to depend on only God and yourself for 2 years? Come on people this is a sign and wonder to bring us back to Him. The veil has been torn, the work has been finished and we can go directly to our God making our request known, speaking to him as Abba Father, basking in His presence, then we will know How to serve Him and others. We have to connect with Him first and keep the connection by continued personal time spent with Him. We should be like Christ by spending time away from everyone in prayer and communing with God. How else was he able to carry out the plan of God in his human body? Well many times we can find Jesus alone and stepping away from the crowds to pray. Just think when he prayed in the Garden of Gethsemane, what a personal time that had to be.

I love that song that says "put your hand in the hand of the man who stilled the waters, put your hand in the hand of the man who calms the sea, take a look at yourself and you can look at others differently, put your hand in the hand of the man from Galilee." We always talk about what Jesus would do or that we follow Jesus when we really don't. We follow doctrines and disguise it as Jesus. NO, we have to stop living in this deceit. We wonder why we have been so powerless and why church has been more painful than healing–

God's Plan

wondering why it has been so consuming of our time, talents and earnings. It has cost us our sanity, our families and our communities. It has weakened our very fiber because we stopped following the examples of Christ. He came to demolish this behavior, break up fallow ground and point us to God. What a rat race the church has become. We have become like a dog chasing its tail–going nowhere and ineffective in the plan of God. Let's stop the madness and turn back to our first love, kneel and pray. If the people who are called by my name would humble themselves and pray and turn back to Me I will heal their land. What do we think this really means? It is clear, how else do we need to translate this message (2 Chronicles 7:14).

Let's talk about the elephant in the room. What has the church done?

We have drained people's time! For people who have families and jobs the church has made it mandatory to be there for anniversary of the church, usher board anniversary, deacon's auxiliary, pastors anniversary, birthdays, wedding anniversary, Sunday service, bible study and the list goes on. Not to mention the dollar amount required for all of these events. When do they have time to spend with God and their families? We are too busy to sit at the feet of Christ to learn more about God and His will! When do we truly have time? What do these things have to do with winning souls? Why do we accept that preacher's kids grow up to be the worst behaving adults? Why is all of this accepted and normalized?

God's Plan

All this produces is tired worn out people, troubled families and marriages, exhausted employees when they go to work. Pastors are sleeping with women, men and children and we keep looking the other way.--giving the excuse that they are people too and we can't expect any more from them. In the church today we see that there is no power, no love, no integrity, no true worship. We also see people dying and literally losing their minds. In this current and sad state some might ask "Where is God?"

This is real and we need to stop before God gives another warning. What's it going to take?

People are seeing all of this and have an 'I don't care attitude' when it comes to the things of God. They do not want to have anything to do with the church.

God's Plan

We have organizations in the church that we treat like they are a sorority or a fraternity and you cannot join unless you are approved. We have totally gotten far away from praying and seeking God's face. What has happened to prayer meetings? We have left praying up to the intercessors with no support. Why are we not utilizing all the gifts God has so generously given to the body? What has happened to morality in the church? We have tension between each other and competing for roles. How are we different from the world? Where is the light, where is the love? Philippians 2:1-4 Therefore if there is any consolation in Christ, if any comfort of love, if any fellowship of the Spirit, if any affection and mercy, fulfill my joy by being of one accord, of one mind. Let nothing be done through selfish ambition or conceit, but in lowliness of mind let each esteem others better than himself. Let each of you look out not only for his own interests, but also the interest of others.

There is still time to get back to the things of God, it will not be easy because there are so many hardened hearts and disturbed minds but if we pray and turn back to God for real this time He will heal us. We have to be accountable and accept responsibility for what we have done. We have to spend time with God in prayer like Christ did. We have to be moved by the Spirit and follow God. Not just the structure of religious repetitive behavior.

It is time for repentance by admitting what we have done, by turning back to God and His ways in love and compassion and not legalism. We need to begin to pray and seek God for only the gain of experiencing His Love and His Will. Study His word not just at church but in a quiet place at home. Pray and teach our families. Once we do this God will renew our minds and cleanse our hearts. We have to face the truth, forgive one another, meet the needs of our brothers and sisters with a motivation of love for God and love for ourselves and others. We have to follow the things that Jesus did he is our great example. Then people will be drawn back to God, they will know us by the love we show to each other and to God. Then we can be a blessing by walking in integrity and love. This should be our motive.

I remember an old song by Andre Crouch that said take me back to the place where I first believed, that place of love for Him when we first believed. Then we will experience God's peace and live in His promises, then His Power and Glory will prevail, not just at church but in our daily lives. There are lost souls out there that need to know how much God loves them

God's Plan

and the only way to reach them is to be examples of God's love, be ambassadors of Kingdom behavior. We do not have to be perfect but we should have a Godly consciousness and have the motivation to walk as Christ did. I beseech you to walk in love for God, love for yourselves and love for others. Be harmless as doves and wise as serpents, be the light that represents our God and how much He loves us. Join Him at His plan for the world. Taking up our cross and walking in our purpose.

We need to ask God to help us walk in the fruits of the spirit (Galatians 5:22). We need to ask for Wisdom. We need to ask what is my purpose? He will answer, James 2:5 If any of you lack wisdom, you should ask God, who gives generously to all without finding fault, and it will be given to you.

God's Plan

A Few Testimonies

For the past year I have been a part of a home bible study that was not planned but came together organically. It is a few ladies and we come together and study the Word of God and share with each other. It has truly been edifying and is a safe place with the only motive being to know God more. It reminds me of the days when the Christ and the Disciples would come together in homes and talk about God and break bread together.

In this regard, I have asked some of the ladies to share their past church experiences.

One of the ladies had the following testimony. "My experience with the church has been relatively good. I was saved at an early age around 10 years old. I had my first encounter with the Holy Spirit which led me to confessing that Jesus was Lord and had died for my sins. I was baptized shortly after and throughout much of my childhood and teenage years I never got involved in any type of ministries, although I did attend vocational bibles school during the summers. I always looked at the members in the church that were involved in ministries as having a closer relationship with God. I guess I never felt worthy enough to pursue my own calling. Once my faith got stronger and my relationship with God became personal I started seeing church in a different way. I really do not like the religious acts of the church doing the same things over and over again as well as it feeling like there were groups of clicks. I had one experience with a church that I would never forget. It was a small church and immediately the pastor's wife was drawn to me. I did serve on the usher board and was very involved however, I have started noticing that I was just

God's Plan

doing things in church being busy but my relationship wasn't personal. This church was extremely religious. They constantly preached about sin which at one point I was questioning my salvation, if I was really saved. I knew it was time to leave and I had to get back spending personal quality time with God to build myself back up from that experience and now I know that I am worthy of all that God has for me regardless of sin in my life I am free and liberated. "

Paul said it best in Galatians 1:6 -10 (NLV) I am shocked that you are turning away so soon from God, who called you to himself through the loving mercy of Christ. You are following a different way that pretends to be the Good News. But it is not the Good News at all. You are being fooled by those who deliberately twist the truth concerning Christ. Let God's curse fall on anyone, including us or even an angel from heaven, who preaches a different kind of Good News than the one we preached to you. I say again what we have said before: if anyone preaches any Good News other than the one you welcomed, let that person be cursed. Obviously, I'm not trying to win the approval of people, but of God. If pleasing people was my goal, I would not be Christ's servant.

Why do we keep people in bondage of sin and feeling not worthy when God already took care of all of this through the finished works of Christ our Savior? Sin is preached over and over and over again until you just forget about the Good News and focus on what you are not doing right. This kind of bondage creates guilt and results in not feeling worthy to serve and pursue God. Teach the Good News and let God work out the plan of Salvation for His people. And yes, it is the responsibility of the church to bring the truth, build them up in the knowledge of Christ (Ephesians 4:13-15)

Another sister stated, "Throughout my childhood, I was moderately involved in my hometown church. I was an usher, altar girl, on the steward board, etc. The social aspect was nice as they had a lot of programs and trips for the kids but I still felt kind of left out. I felt there was favoritism shown to certain people/families and I was acutely aware of it, at a young age. It wasn't until I entered my teen years that I truly felt like the black sheep and felt uncomfortable in the church. I couldn't quite put my finger on it at the time, but when I became older there was an underlying feeling of "it's my way or the highway" with our aging preacher and his family. Anyone that opposed their "rule" or point of view endured the consequences and repercussions and our membership slowly dwindled, as a result.

When I was old enough to choose whether I went to church or not, I stopped going. When I moved to Georgia I attempted to go to other churches but still never felt comfortable and never stayed long. I remember attending a Bible study with a prophet and he basically blamed women who experienced rape stating that they put themselves in situations and wore revealing clothing. I still regret never standing and saying something to correct him. But I couldn't believe he had the nerve to be a representative of God spouting such terrible things so I never went back to that or any church since.

This weekly Bible study, running for almost a year, was surprising for me. It was at one session that I learned the truth that God is love and he wants us to experience Him. Not as the church would have you believe that we're too condemned to feeling guilt and shame for being imperfect and falling short of God's grace and mercy. Because honestly that's really the words I associate with church. Guilt, shame and judgment. Bible study has made developing a relationship with God seem more accessible. I never felt that was prior. And I feel more encouraged to read the Bible for myself and as a lifelong process instead of something that you just read through and be done with like any other book."

What an awesome testimony, the most exciting thing is she has a thirst to know God and has the confidence that God loves her. She knows God has begun a work in her and will continue no matter what.

I have heard all the excuses in the church such as if they want a perfect church don't join or if it is a personal thing we need to go to God. It is so funny to me that whenever a person

God's Plan

questions the church or its leaders that is when we want to tell them to go to God. If a person does not find church to be a place of safety, where they can be edified, loved and built up in the knowledge of Christ then there is a problem.

Another sister stated "When I was a child I was actively involved in religious services. I most definitely participated in the praise team, assisted with feeding the kids after the service, and served as an usher when required. I was always instructed to dress modestly by wearing long gowns and tams.

Our church was inclusive and diverse. Numerous multicultural families from Bahamas, Jamaica, Guyana, and Hati joined and grew very close to one another. I vividly remember our summer school sessions, which were quite educational and enjoyable, and

God's Plan

which gave me the foundation for studying more about God's word. We all felt a sense of family and enjoyed being around one another.

I can keep grounded during the week thanks to our weekly bible study. This is a refueling source of my faith and my understanding of God's word. As a future Christian, I can state that a midweek boost is important, especially when I'm feeling down. This also helps me to create meaningful connections with God's people. We were meant to depend on God first, but also on each other. This group also provides a safe space for us to share our grief, struggles and pain. It also gives us the opportunity to comfort those in distress, and deep sorrow. I am truly delighted to be a part of this group that has nourished my spiritual thirst."

God's Plan

This is an example of a person who has enjoyed her younger years of service and belonging in a church but what about after she became an adult. What did the church have to offer her besides service? These are real times with real challenges in life. Do we offer true discipleship?

Another person shared her experience with the church, "I was introduced to church as a little girl and loved to dress up in beautiful dresses and matching socks. I attended youth services, bible studies, prayer meetings and participated as a praise and worship leader. I also went to a Christian college, my mom made sure I was in every church service growing up. I felt well equipped with the Word. However, when in college and life began to happen I began drifting away. Not only from God but from church. When I did go to church I found it to be manipulative and misleading. I said I know

God's Plan

that no one is perfect but I found myself angry and did not want to be involved. I totally dropped off and did not care anymore.

Now attending the bible study has made me excited again, and I feel the blind spots in my thinking has been corrected. My perspective has changed, even after growing up in church I did not understand the significance of having a relationship with God. "This experience has not only been an eye opener but a mind opener. I am amazed that when we study the Bible together it magically creates meaningful connections and provides the necessary encouragement by enriching me as I hear the Word. It keeps me accountable by helping me comprehend the biblical truth and how to apply it. Also it helps direct me to wisdom. I would say the Bible is our roadmap for life and I believe that sometimes we need help to read a map and can benefit from someone else's experience in God's work. Studying the Bible has provided me with insights that I hadn't yet learned. It provided powerful means that made it exciting to see the beauty of journeying through the Bible together. I found it to be transformational, and I look forward to fellowship. It's gotten to a point that when I miss a meeting I feel empty. The Word just knows how to fill me up and keep me motivated and going."

Several thoughts here, when our college students leave, what kind of support do we offer? Do we have someone available for them to call and check to see how they are doing or to ask questions or just to discuss the Word of God? We do not need some on-campus big event that ties them to the church but, instead, just true discipleship. Also, do we promote to the children that attending church and youth events are great but you must also seek God

God's Plan

when you are not here. You need to pray and talk to God and read the Word to keep the personal relationship going. Why don't we teach our young children about having a relationship with God? Especially nowadays since children are so bright so early in life we should be bringing them up in the true knowledge of God so they will not depart from it. Instead we make them feel guilty and ashamed. Children should always leave our presence feeling edified.

God's Plan

Message to Leaders

Manipulation is another area of concern within the church. Why do we use the church as a tool of manipulation in the first place? Any time you promote people to give out of pressure or duress you are using manipulation to intimidate people to give of their time, talent or finances. The Bible tells us not to give under duress and to be happy givers and not to give so much that we don't have. (2nd Corithians 8:11-14) We have to stop using the tithe and offering as a means of punishment from God if we do not give. It is wrong in so many ways. How do you become a free giver? You teach the word as it is written, build them up in the knowledge, encourage personal time with God then they will grow to the maturity in their relationship with God to do His will. We need to stop selling fear, God did not give us the spirit of fear but love, a strong mind and power. (2nd

Timothy 1:7). When you teach the Word of God in itself it will become alive in people.

We have to stop tickling the ear's of the people of God just to get an emotional response from them. We have to stop letting church just be a place to come and shout and scream with no permanent impact on our personal lives. We have a church full of people who will run, shout and scream but after that is over with we go back to our mean, selfish and harmful ways. There is no love, no true discipleship, and this cycle continues. The bottom line is that God loves us all, he has forgiven us all through the finished works of His only begotten son. Now we have to demonstrate what we say we believe and who we say we serve. We do this by showing love in the most difficult times, we do this by obeying God regardless of what we want to do or say or what it looks like. Does it not say to Love our neighbors as ourselves,

God's Plan

does it not say obedience is better than sacrifice?

Leaders, spend quality time with God, get in your quiet place every day and be silent before the Lord, seek His heart and He will show you great and mighty things, He will direct you and reward you. He will show you how to lead His people.

Did God not say pray without ceasing, did He not say eye has not seen ear has not heard what He is going to show us, did not His word say he would be a lamp unto our feet and a light unto our path?

Trust in the Lord with all your heart and lean not to your own understanding, in all your ways acknowledge Him and He shall direct your path (Proverbs 3:5-6).

God's Plan

Do you believe him to the point that you are going to do it your way or the way of this world or the way you were taught? Be careful God's people to not confuse your will with His.

These are His people not yours, these are sheep He has given you not authority over but to watch over like a Shepherd watches over His sheep. Making sure they are safe, fed and well taken care of. That is your job. Teach if you are called to teach but keep God first in all you do. Preach if this is what God has called you to do but keep God first in all you do. You are accountable for every sheep He has given you, not to control and manipulate but to guide them back to God by equipping them. Fasting, praying and being in a quiet place will keep your heart connected to the true power and not our own power.

God's Plan

Seek ye first the kingdom of God and all these things shall be added unto you. Do not burden the people with taking care of you. God is your resource, does He not take care of the lilies? How much more does He think of you? Stop living in fear of losing and know that God is on your side, choose Him and watch the salvation of the Lord manifest in your life and all the lives around you. Don't be afraid of who will not accept you or who will reject you. Nothing will ever separate you from the love of God. Allow me to remind you He will never leave you or forsake you. He is the Alpha and Omega The Great I Am, Our Lord, Elohim, full of loving kindness and His mercy is everlasting and His truth endures forever.

What God has for you is for you. Hold to God's unchanging hand and build your hopes on things eternal. I say again hold to God's unchanging hand.

God's Plan

Freedom from Fear

We have had enough of fear, let's live in the assurance of the finished work of Christ. Let's live in the liberty God has so mercifully given us. Let's go back to the joy of the Lord being our strength. Let's go back to being and living in the grace God has provided for us. We have had enough fear taught to us and God's word says He has not given us the spirit of Fear but of love power and a strong mind. Let us take fear out of the equation of decision-making. Fear and caution are 2 different things, God will give you the wisdom to make decisions that are based on His will for our lives and others. Trust in the Lord with all your heart and lean not to your own understanding but in all your ways acknowledge Him and he shall direct your path. Acknowledging God is doing His will, loving those who are even hard to love and includes serving His people and

God's Plan

taking care of our families. Let us realign our minds and efforts with the heart to serve God in every way He sets forth for us. Let the motivation always be to serve Him and others with Love.

Demonstration as a Tool

We need to understand that demonstration is a powerful tool. The word says you will know them by the fruit they bear (Luke 6:43-45). We need to demonstrate the fruits of the Spirit so others can see God (Galatians 5:22-23). The Word also says be doers and not just hearers, people will know us by how we treat each other. All of these are demonstrations of Kingdom living. We need to individually ask ourselves "what do people see in me?" We should pray, God show me anything that is in my heart that is not like you please remove it so your light can be seen. We need to stand for morality, integrity, and love at all times. Sometimes it is not easy however, God will help us get there but we have to be intentional. Did not the word say seek ye first the kingdom of God and His righteousness? Are we actively working towards righteousness or are we

God's Plan

settling for "Oh this is me this is how I am and God's going to have to change me? If you have a problem with me, take it to Jesus. This is not intentionally seeking and doing what God has commanded from us. He says to Love each other that means serving each other with humility that can say I am sorry for the way I have acted towards you, humility that says I will look beyond the fault and see the need and humility that says how can I serve?

Loveless Church

Revelations 2 says I know your works, your labor, your patience and that you cannot bear those who are evil. And you have tested those who say they are apostles and are not and have found them liars and you have preserved and have been patient and have labored for My name's sake and have not become weary. Nevertheless I have this against you, that you have left your first love. Remember therefore from where you have fallen: repent and do the first works, or else I will come to you quickly and remove your lampstand from its place unless you repent.

He who has an ear, let him hear what the Spirit is saying to us.

God's Plan

My Prayer

I pray that everyone will stop and hear what Our God is saying in this season. I pray we'll all allow our hearts to be examined and that we are willing to change. I pray that we open our hearts and minds to the things of God. I pray that we become one with Him in Love and become true Ambassadors of the Kingdom of God. That we love God with all our hearts, soul and mind, that we love our neighbor as ourselves. That we become consumed with the plan of God and it be the only motive in our hearts in Jesus Name Amen.

Prayer of Repentance

Some of us are afraid of the word Repentance because of the way it has been taught. For me, I have been afraid of the word because I thought it meant you will not sin again and there was also a condemnation attached to it. But now I know the true meaning of repentance, it simply means you recognize God's way and want to join Him by acknowledging His way in my actions and thoughts and asking God to help you to change your heart. It can be over night but sometimes there are layers of healing that need to happen before you get to the place you desire to be. It is a true remorse of wanting to change and having a strong determination to join God in your behavior.

God's Plan

With that said, God gave me a prayer of repentance and if you feel the need after reading this book to repent feel free to pray the prayer below. This book is not to condemn you for there is no condemnation for those who are in Christ Jesus who desire to walk not after the flesh but after the Spirit (Romans 8:1).

We repent Dear God for taking matters into our own hands, for forgetting and mocking you with our pride, agendas and evil hearts. We have taken your good name in vain and made a mockery of it by not representing you as true ambassadors of your Kingdom. We took matters into our own hands. We did not wait for you to speak before we moved forward, we took your Kingdom into our own hands. We did not display love and compassion for your people. We ask for forgiveness, for your word tells if we confess our sins you are faithful and just and will forgive us and cleans us from all unrighteousness (1 John 1:8-9). We will love one another so the world will know your love and see that we are true disciples of the cross and what it represents (John 13:35). We thank you for Freedom from sin, freedom from the world's ways and desires. We thank you for liberty to live and breathe and have our being in you because of the finished works of Jesus Christ our Savior who is our great example.

Hallelujah, thine are the Glory and the Power and Dominion over all and in all! Thank you that I can declare that I am the Righteousness of God through faith Amen!